Capturing Your Story

Capturing Your Story
Writing a memoir step by step

Gloria VanDemmeltraadt

Copyright 2017 by Gloria VanDemmeltraadt
All rights reserved. No part of this book may be reproduced in any form or by any means, electronic or mechanical, including photocopying, recording, or by any information storage and retrieval system, without written permission from the author.

ISBN: 978-0-9908375-1-0
Library of Congress Number: 2017945527

Printed in the United States of America

Cover & interior design by FuzionPrint.com

21 20 19 18 17   5 4 3 2 1

Capturing Your Story

Writing a memoir step by step

Table of Contents

Introduction 1

Chapter 1
    What Is a Memoir? 5

Chapter 2
    Why Write Your Story – Either as a Life Story, a Memoir, or an Autobiography? 11
    Who is it for 12
    Target Market 14

Chapter 3
    How Do I Start: 19
    What's the First Step? 23

Chapter 4
    Here's Another Approach 29
    Exercise 31

Chapter 5
    Diagram Your Life....................................... 37

Chapter 6
    The Narrative Arc.. 47

Chapter 7
    Finding the Story or Plot in a Memoir 53

Chapter 8
    Editing 61

Chapter 9
    Naming Your Story 67
    Cover and Design 68

Chapter 10
    Build your Writing Muscle 73

Chapter 11
    How to Publish/Print Your Story 79

Chapter 12
    Good Luck and Keep Writing 85

Introduction

"You don't write because you want to say something, you write because you have something to say."
—F. Scott Fitzgerald

Yes, everyone has something to say! The fact that someone has lived to be the age they are, whatever that may be, is a story in itself. Experience, environment, and temperament are different for every person in this world. The memories related to all of these factors are important to future generations, and my goal is to help people understand how to capture those memories.

Who am I – and what makes me qualified to help others learn how to write about their memories?

I am a woman with a passion for helping others capture their stories. Above all, I am a hospice volunteer, working with patients to write their stories. I have done more than a hundred of these stories – and it is the most exciting, rewarding, and wonderful thing I do. The look on each patient's face is priceless when they hold their very own story in their hands, and this is true of family, too.

I see myself as a searcher or an investigator – trying to draw out people's memories, mainly for the joy and comfort for family, and also so that next generations will understand how life was for their loved one.

I have also lived through a wide and rocky variety of life experiences.

Singing was my love until I lost my hearing and turned to writing, which has now brought me much joy. For my husband and me, learning to laugh after many tragedies has been an astonishing reawakening and we both cherish each day we have.

I have written and published three books, *Musing and Munching* is my own story telling memories of my tumultuous young adult life as they relate to food, or lack of it, and half of the book is a cookbook. The second, *Memories of Lake Elmo*, is the history of the village of Lake Elmo, Minnesota, told in the stories of more than 120 people interviewed, plus a great deal of research I did about the town. The third, *Darkness in Paradise*, is the story of my current husband's life as a child during the Japanese occupation of the Dutch East Indies during World War II. It is an unusual look at WWII, written with humor and wonder as viewed through a child's eyes. It follows his path from where he was born in the Dutch East Indies which became Indonesia, to Holland, back to Indonesia and again to Holland, and more.

Thanks for making this book possible go to many. Thanks especially to members of WOW (Women of Words) for encouragement and support, as well as their amazing talents in physically getting it edited, proofread, and published. Thanks go to the dozens of people who have attended my presentations over the past several years in hopes of being inspired to write their stories. I am thrilled to say that many have done so or are in the process, and I couldn't be happier. Most of all, thank you to my friends and family who continue to inspire me daily and whose love makes life a joy.

I am determined to help others capture their memories. I work hard to provide the best, most clear, and sensible information I can put together to inspire and motivate *you* to begin the process of capturing your memories. Let's begin!

Chapter 1

What Is a Memoir?

People often ask what is the difference between a biography, an autobiography, and a memoir. A biography is a story of a person's life, but written by someone other than the one whose life is described. An autobiography is the self-told story of a person's life.

A memoir is about a certain point in time. It can be about significant parts of a person's life, such as a troubled childhood. It could be a specific time when the person is unusually happy, such as telling about feelings and events surrounding a wedding or the birth of a child. It could be about time spent traveling, of going to school, or any specific period in a person's life.

A memoir can also be a story about a characteristic of a person's life. For example, Patricia Hampl is called the "Queen of Memoir," having written four so far. She says you can write a dozen memoirs or more, depending on how you capture a special moment or a memory, or an aspect of a character. Her most recent memoir, *The Florist's Daughter*, is simply about forgiveness. Hampl says,

> *"Memoir is not what happened. It is what has happened over time, in the mind, in the life as it attends to these tantalizing, dismaying, broken bits of life history. It is a try at the truth – the truth of a self in the world."*

Another form of personal writing is known as "legacy letters," or "Ethical Wills." These are merely a short form of a memoir or autobiography or life story. They contain a synopsis of a person's life that might contain these things:

- Beginning:
  - Who are you and how did you come to be born where you were?
  - Who are your ancestors?
- What is your story? A short version of what you've done with your life.
- What have you learned? Share who you really are, via your values and beliefs, your life's lessons.
- Thanks:
  - Express your love and concern for the ones you care about.
  - Forgiving others and asking for forgiveness.

Capturing Your Story

"Grief journaling" is another form of writing and helps people work their way through grief over a death or other kind of loss. This sort of writing, which is extremely personal as well as therapeutic, is not usually meant to be shared. It can, however, be a satisfying and healing path to dealing with a painful loss.

Tips from this publication can help in guiding someone who doesn't yet know how, but wants to capture their experiences and feelings connected with their loss, without sharing the resulting writings with others.

A time to reflect

Jot down some notes, doodle, reflect...

Memories

Chapter 2

Why Write Your Story – Either as a Life Story, a Memoir, or an Autobiography?

When we're young, no one wants to think about death or becoming infirm. That's how life is. As we age – or our parents get older and begin to have difficulties and start slowing down – niggling thoughts begin to sneak into our minds. "What if something happens to Mom?"

One of the saddest declarations I've heard is: "I wish I had asked my mother about her young life. I don't know anything about her life before I came along. Or my father, or my grandmother, or my grandfather."

My goal is for you to begin capturing your own memories for *your* next generation.

You haven't told your loved ones about your life or what they mean to you, or what you hope from them. Just imagine if something happens when you go on a vacation or a business trip, or maybe overnight somewhere, and you don't come back?

The first questions to ask yourself about why to write a story are:
- Have you had a significant event or situation in your lifetime that you want to share?
- Have others suggested that you write your story? Maybe it was your child or other relative or friend.
- Do you want to capture your memories overall, or just a piece of them?
- What is your central viewpoint or philosophy, and why do you want to share it?

A poignant quote from Dr. Seuss reads:

"Sometimes you will never know the value of a moment until it becomes a memory."

Who is it for?

Who do you think would like to read your story? Would it be family, friends, or only you? Sometimes a memoir or life story can be a catharsis or a cleansing way to write down – and heal from – bad memories. It's good to pour a hurtful story onto paper and the very act of writing it can get emotions into a solid form, for you to think about, to study, and to release. However, thinking about who is going to read those emotions is critical in refining what you keep in your story, but also

Capturing Your Story

what you might write, and then decide to delete, for various reasons.

Is your story for your family only, or do you hope to publish it for others? Deciding will have a profound effect and helps determine how you will publish or print your story when you finish. Will it be in story-form or book-form? Thinking about it upfront will help in how you begin to write and collect memories for your story. This is discussed in more detail at the end of this booklet.

It's important to know who will be your audience, and requires honest and realistic thought. For example, when I wrote my own memoir, it began with my children asking me to write down the "farm stories" for our family to enjoy. We had lived on a hobby farm for a number of years, and had many hilarious and a few not-so-fun experiences there.

As I began capturing the stories, more memories flooded in. When the story was finished, others who read it thought this was more than simply a story for my family, and urged me to make it a book for others to enjoy and learn from. It morphed from a story for my own family, to become a lesson in perseverance and determination for others dealing with issues of neglect and mistreatment.

This sort of segue from simply writing a story to writing a book can happen, and it is certainly a possibility to keep in mind. It's important, from the

beginning, to consider for whom you are writing. The audience can grow, as mine did, but the focus should start with defining your goals for your writing in general. So ask yourself:
- Why are you writing?
- What is your central viewpoint or philosophy, and why do you want to share it?
- Who will listen to what you have to say?

Target Market

From Wikipedia®: "A target market is a group of customers a business has decided to aim its marketing efforts and ultimately its merchandise toward. A well-defined target market is the first element of a marketing strategy. Product, price, promotion, and place are the four elements of a marketing mix strategy that determine the success of a product or service in the marketplace."

Basically, the target market for your story or book is the people you expect will buy and read it.

Saying your book is for "everybody" is too broad, and it's important to define a more specific audience.

A story that will appeal to the over-50 generation may not be current or interesting enough for millennials, or teenagers and twenty-somethings.

To illustrate the effect of determining your audience, imagine you're writing a letter to your grandmother about going to your high school senior prom. What might you include, and what might you leave out? Then, write on the same topic to your best friend, and think about the differences in the letters. Keeping your audience in mind as you write will help you make good decisions about what to include, and how to organize your ideas.

Continue asking yourself:

- What am I trying to say with this story?
- Who am I trying to help and to reach?

Jeanette Walls, American writer and journalist, says:

"Memoir is about handing over your life to someone and saying, this is what I went through, this is who I am, and maybe you can learn something from it. It's honestly sharing what you think, feel, and have gone through."

Doing that successfully gives others the understanding and advantage of your experience without having to live it, themselves.

A time to reflect

Jot down some notes, doodle, reflect…

Memories

Chapter 3

How Do I Start?

In one of my former business lives, I was a communications consultant with an engineering firm. I administered the Myers Briggs Type Indicator and other style instruments to determine the various personality types of those who worked together.

I mention this because people have different ways of gaining energy, taking in information, making decisions, and living our lives.

"Truth" then, is different according to who heard or saw it. Think about stories we've heard about accidents and other public incidents where everyone interviewed says something different about the same event. One person might tell the tiniest details, but not be aware of the overall picture of what happened.

For example, here are two views of eyewitnesses to a car crash: the first person says, "I saw this gray-haired man standing on the corner, and he had a puzzled look on his face. One of his shoelaces was untied, and as he looked down at his shoe, his cap slipped down over his nose, and suddenly a car almost hit him." Another person says about the same situation, "I saw a car going fast and the next thing I knew, it hit another car and almost hit some people."

The bottom line is: We don't see the world as it is, we see the world as *we are*. It is important to understand that we are individuals, and others may not be like us. Others are not wrong, they are just different.

There's a quote that is credited to Albert Einstein, but it's disputed whether he really said it. In any event, it's a great line and fits here.

> *"Everyone is a genius, but if you keep judging a fish on its ability to climb a tree, it will always think it's stupid."*

We are all different.

A disclaimer, or preface, or something at the beginning of a memoir is important to explain that this is *your* story, or *your* version of your truth in the world. If you identify that upfront, you're usually okay, because invariably, it is going to differ from someone else's view.

For example, in my own memoir, my sister, who is older by 11 years, disagreed completely with my description of our father. She had grown up with a father who was a farmer, home all the time, and didn't drink. When I came along, our father was working odd hours and going to bars every night, and became a mean alcoholic for a time. We grew up in totally different situations, and couldn't relate to the same man being our father.

Some people have better memories and thus can remember their childhoods in more clarity and detail than others. This has become clear to me as I work with hospice patients on their stories. Some remember times with their grandparents and even great-grandparents in amazing detail, and we are able to capture priceless memories for their families, which would otherwise never have been known.

A recent church sermon sparked some good discussion with friends, and clarified another difference in how people think and gather memories. It was about life's journeys and destinations. Do you focus strictly on getting to a destination, or do you appreciate the beauties of the journey along the way?

I must admit to being what is known as a Type A personality: outgoing, ambitious, impatient, and focused. Type B personalities, including my husband, are more relaxed and enjoy the game, rather than winning.

Type A folks are often too focused on getting to their destination instead of enjoying the journey and its branches and spinoffs that lead them to that destination.

Knowing our own preferences and lifestyle helps greatly to understand how we can be complemented by another's viewpoint, and it adds significantly to remembering the journeys along life's path.

There are countless different ideas about how to write a memoir; each of course is dictated by the individual's personal preferences.

William Zinsser, another memoirist, says, "Writers are the custodians of memory," and that's what you must become if you want to leave some kind of record of your life and of the family you were born into. That record can take many shapes, and it can be:

- A formal memoir—a vigilant piece of strict scholarly construction.
- An informal family history, written to tell your children and your grandchildren about the family they were born into.
- An oral history that you capture by tape or video recorder.
- Anything else you want it to be: some hybrid mixture of history and reminiscence.

Whatever it is, it's an important kind of writing. Too often memories die with their owner, without having been captured on paper or any other way, and too often time surprises us by running out.

Only *you* can tell the story you've lived, and other people's lives will be deepened for it.

What's the First Step?

Many sources for memoir writing suggest making lists. This method works especially well for people who prefer structure in their lives, and see themselves as sensible and prepared.

1. Start by making a list of all the important dates and events in your life. Check old records to ensure the information you are providing is accurate. Don't dwell on too many details at first; you can always go back to finish things later.
2. Jog your memory by reading old journals or diary entries, or letters.
3. Look at old photos. Who's there, who is not, where was it taken, what was the occasion, and when was it, what was the weather like ...
    - Kate Morton in *The Lake House* – a great summer read – essentially used one photo for the basis of a whole book. This one was fiction; a novel, not a non-fictional memoir, but the concept is the same. She talked about the lines in her father's face; what caused them, was it shell shock from the war, or what? The stuffed toy in the little boy's hand; where is it now? Mother's dress had a stain on it; was it blood from somebody's cut? The scab on the daughter's knee; what caused it?

4. Begin writing *after* you gather your information. When you write, you should try to focus on the big stories rather than technical details. Provide important dates, but don't go into great detail about the less important stuff until later.

A time to reflect

Jot down some notes, doodle, reflect...

Memories

Chapter 4

Here's Another Approach

Instead of making lists, try writing memories. It's important to think small. Forget about creating a brilliant epic story that will sweep the country. This will only scare you with the overall magnitude of it all. Instead, make smaller goals.

Sit down in a coffee shop or at your desk, or on your back patio, and start writing a well-defined memory as a short story. It can be any length, even a paragraph, but needs to have a beginning and an end. Put the story away in a folder, and tomorrow write another one. Write your way through your life, one memory at a time, until you have a bulging folder, real or digital.

Then, either print them all out or look at all the stories on your computer using a multiple page view. Read through the stories to see which pieces work with others, and patterns will form as you move the stories around.

Now, your job is to put it all together. As you organize the stories, it will become clear as to what your memoir is about, and what it is not about.

Using this method is like putting together a huge jigsaw puzzle. You will see what fits in one spot might not fit in another. It will show you where empty spots are, where you need to fill in another story or make a transition to another time period.

I love this quote from Mark Twain about writing a memoir:

"Start at no particular time in your life; wander at your free will all over your life."

An event doesn't have to be huge to build a whole story or even a book around it. It's the *impact* of a moment or an event.

An example could be going to the zoo with your grandfather. This could lead to a lifetime of loving animals, or the reverse: a lifetime of fearing cats, or snakes, or anything else.

In general, ask yourself specific questions, like:
- What is your earliest memory?
- What was it like to shave your legs for the first time?
- How did you learn to drive?
- When did you first use makeup?
- Were you ever in a parade?

- Did you ever get gum in your hair?
- What games did you play with your friends when you were very young?
- Describe a game you made up.
- Who was your best teacher and why?
- What is your favorite food and who made/makes it?

Thinking of events or moments like this leads to lots of ideas or memories for stories.

Above all, tell the truth. *A memoir is what really happened.* So, using dialog is a gray area because nobody remembers exactly the words used in conversations from long ago, but when dialog flows from memory, it is often spot on.

My mother gave me some wonderful advice that is burned into my mind. She said,

"Always tell the truth. When you make something up or tell a lie, you always have to remember what you said. When you tell the truth, it's automatic, and just flows out of you without conscious remembering."

Exercise

Thinking about writing a real memory, it's time to do a short exercise.

Choose one of these sentences or topics, and write for five minutes about it. Try to write with feelings and

emotions, and not just tell only what happened. You might get only a paragraph written, and that's okay.
- It was fall (spring, summer, winter) and ...
- I couldn't stop smiling when ....
- In that moment, everything changed.
- My greatest challenge was ...
- What are you sorry you never did?
- What physical characteristic are you proud to pass on?
- When did you unexpectedly feel compassion?

Set your timer and start writing. When the timer dings, stop writing. Now read through your story, and then put it in your physical or electronic folder. You could very well already have a beginning to your memoir. Doing this short but powerful action every day will put you well on the way to a collection of stories that will help to define what your memoir is about ... and what it's not about. It will show you where to go next, what's important to you, and what's not. It will bring out your own personal style and tone of writing, and it will most certainly be the truth.

You don't need to tell your story chronologically, although that's the easiest way of writing an autobiography or a memoir. Think of your favorite books. Most don't start at the beginning. Instead, they grab you with instant action and intrigue. A good beginning is a tease. It's also called a "hook." It gives readers enough action to hook them without revealing the outcome. Then the story can flash back to the real chronological beginning, and you can fill in the background.

Look at the short story you wrote for this exercise that answered one of the questions or statements listed. Many times, when I've used this exercise in a class on writing a memoir, in the short five minutes allowed, participants come up with the perfect way or hook, to start their memoir. You don't always need to pressure yourself with a timer when you write, but for this short exercise, it acts as a shove to get you started.

A time to reflect

Jot down some notes, doodle, reflect...

Memories

Chapter 5

Diagram Your Life

Pictures are another way to look at your life, and for some people, work better than outlining and lists. Many authors use a variety of ways to diagram a life. I suggest these two: a Physical Diagram and a Conceptual Diagram.

For the Physical Diagram, put YOU (or ME) at the center, and surround yourself with the people and events that have helped to shape your life. Rearrange and work with the diagram to make it reflect your own life. Write all over it, using pencil or sticky notes you can move around if needed. If you think of other connections that affect your life, add them to your expanding diagram as needed.

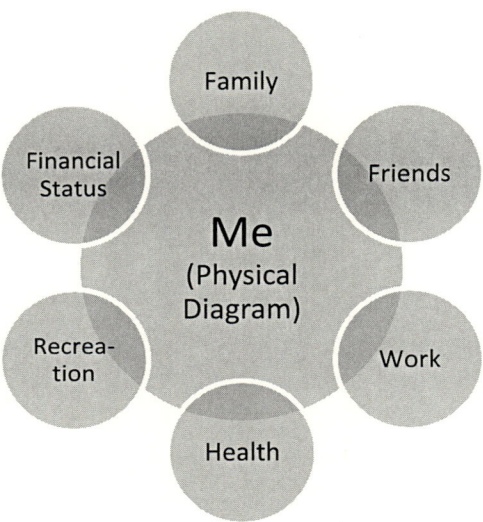

For the Conceptual Diagram, try dividing your life by important choices, significant people, conflicts, beliefs, morals, mistakes you've made, and lessons you've learned. Draw the diagram, and fill in the concepts according to your own experiences. Again, add those concepts that might be missing from the diagram. Experiment and write or draw all over it until you believe it describes you to a T. This will help to refine your life to the stories that perfectly pertain to you.

Capturing Your Story

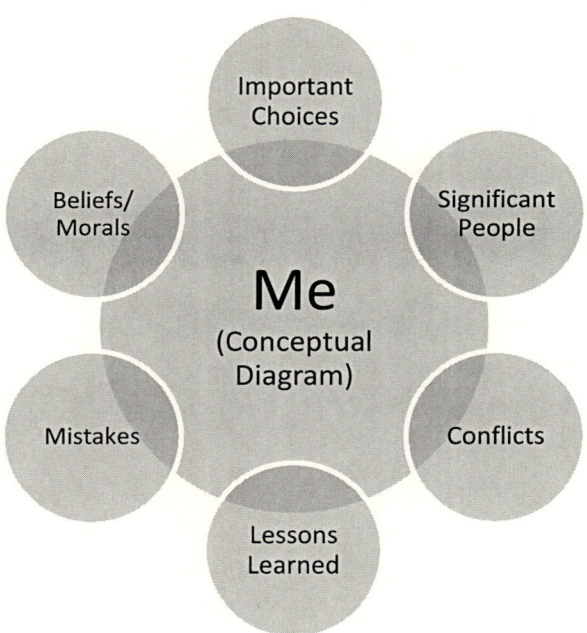

This is only a beginning. You can diagram a life in many different ways, depending on what works for you. Again, experimenting with the diagrams and their contents will help to define the characteristics that describe and make up the miracle that is YOU.

So what method did I use when I wrote my own memoir?

I'm basically a list maker, so I did start that way. I made a list of notable events and happenings in my life. I gathered pictures and random journal entries I had made through the years, and then I started organizing them and building them into stories.

I also gathered some stories I had written years ago and built them into my narrative if they fit and helped to advance the story.

An example here is a story I wrote in a 30-minute college essay exam. It actually became the basis for my own memoir.

It was early fall; a lonely and frightening time for my two little boys and me. Their daddy had left us the winter before when I told him I was pregnant. He said he didn't want to be married anymore.

I don't remember much of spring or summer that year. It was more a matter of getting through it all. The new house in the country was sold, Daddy went to California with somebody else, hurts were hidden, and life went on. We ended up in a dreary apartment above somebody's house in town.

We sat outside on the steps a lot. Just being together, those two little scared-faced boys and me. I worked in an office and they went to a sitter all day, so our short time at night was special. We prayed a lot for Daddy to come back.

I've often wondered about those prayers. Some time later I met a woman whose husband was dying. She was torn between praying for him to die and be at peace, or for him to live and not leave her. She was tormented by the struggle of what to pray for and her agony was painful to see. Finally, a kind person suggested she pray for herself instead, to give her the strength to accept whatever happened. This simple suggestion changed everything. The terrible weight went off her and she bore the coming days with a wonderful peace.

I had no such kind friend and kept on praying for my husband's return. He did not come back and our lives spiraled down in miserable suffering.

Finally, in the fall, my beautiful little girl was born. In true miracle fashion, though a painful and scary time it was, I brought home a healthy, happy little sister, for two, not much older, but world-wise big brothers. From the start she belonged to them. And they all belonged to me.

It wasn't easy, of course. Just getting through the chores involved with a job, a car, an apartment, and four people kept us all running. It was hard to remember they were children, and tiny ones at that, as much as I expected of them.

One morning in the midst of the normal rush the baby fell over and bumped her head. Paul said Mark pushed her. I started yelling at Mark to say he was sorry, all the while dashing around bundling everyone up in scarves and mittens and mufflers to meet the cold outside the door. I repeated again and again, "Say it - go on, say it! Aren't you sorry you hurt your little sister?"

How cruel I was. That confused little four year old boy was terrified of his mother at that moment, but determined to do what was expected. I ranted on, "Say it!" Finally, just as we were ready to pile in the car, Mark looked up at me with fear widened eyes hoping against hope he was doing the right thing and said in a tiny voice, "It."

When I realized what he tried to do and what he really said, all the anger and hurt and exasperation of months of fear and anxiety came pouring out in my tears and laughter, and theirs.

We never went to work that day. We sat on the step and watched the leaves and hugged each other. We sang songs and laughed, and hugged each other some more. And we didn't pray again for Daddy to come home.

Unfortunately, I have never been committed enough to really keep a faithful daily diary. I envy those who do. In searching my earlier writings, I found a number of diaries I had started with good intentions, but dropped after only a day or two.

You who do keep a diary or journal have a wealth of valuable information and memories at your fingertips. This is a priceless source of information and a perfect basis to start your memoir.

A time to reflect

Jot down some notes, doodle, reflect...

Memories

Chapter 6

The Narrative Arc

Every story must have a beginning, a middle, and an end[1]. We can blame Aristotle, or classical Greek culture if we must, but that's the bottom line.

It is called "The Narrative Arc," and all writing must adhere to the format in order to develop a story that will appeal to readers.

Non-fiction writing can easily revert to become a boring recital of one event after another, without adhering to the narrative arc. Writers may think because it's based on what they consider interesting experiences, or historical events or amazing observations, they don't need a plan or a plot to write their story. Sit down and think again.

---

[1] From Wikipedia®: In his "Poetics," the Greek philosopher Aristotle, put forth the idea that, "A whole is what has a beginning and middle and end."

In 1863, the German playwright and novelist Gustav Freytag laid out what has come to be known as Freytag's Pyramid.

Under Freytag's Pyramid, the plot of a story consists of five parts: exposition (beginning or explanation), rising action, climax, falling action, and dénouement (resolution/revelation/end).

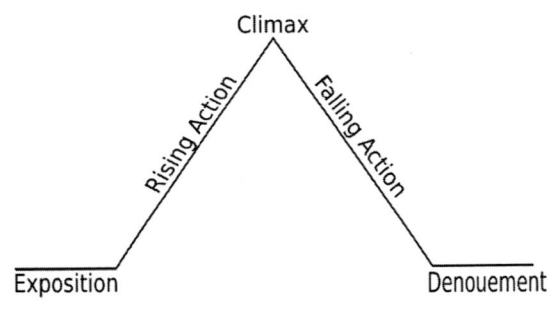

Freytag's Pyramid

Another way to organize a story via the narrative arc is to diagram it on the simple arc below.

Write your beginning and end point of the story, which enclose events in the middle. One of those events can be the highpoint, or climax of the story.

Capturing Your Story

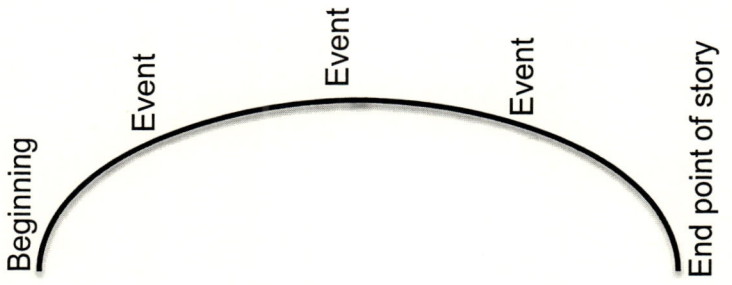

A time to reflect

Jot down some notes, doodle, reflect...

Memories

Chapter 7

Finding the Story or Plot in a Memoir

Writing a memoir or life story is writing a narrative with the storyteller as a character. It is the writer's story, but that does not mean this sort of writing, which is non-fiction, can exist without a plot.

What is a plot? A plot is a series of events showing how the story's characters encounter difficulties and challenges, and how they solve their problems. The subject of the narrative, the protagonist or the central character or hero, is different by the end of the story than he/she is at the beginning.

In addition, something has to tie the work together. The storyteller needs to convince an audience this is a tale worth caring about.

When looking for a plot to the story, try to find the significance of an event, series of events, or a lifestyle. Otherwise, the reader may not understand why this memoir was written in the first place.

This means sitting down and trying to figure out, in a sentence or two, what the memoir is about. If the point of the work can be described in this short and succinct way, then the story has a plot and a point. If not, then there isn't a clear story to the memoir.

For example, my own memoir can be summed up by this sentence: "This book contains stories of my life as they relate to food – or the lack of food – at critical times throughout the years."

It's a simple sentence describing the focus of the work. Rather than having a haphazard collection of memories and stories, they must be connected in a way that leads the reader to want to know more about the stories that are being told.

A man who had invented many interesting gadgets and devices asked me to write up his story. He was a curious person and from childhood on, he experimented with contraptions to make things easier to do. His story was called, "A Lifetime of New Ideas," and that simple phrase perfectly describes the plot of his memoir.

Another example is a woman who was bullied as a child because of her weight. Her story's plot pulled together accounts of how she coped and overcame feelings of depression and poor self-worth.

I worked with a woman who believed she had "gypsy blood." Her story became a fascinating account

Capturing Your Story

from that viewpoint. It told how her gypsy blood made her different from others, giving her flashing eyes, and led her on dancing travels throughout her life.

Finding the plot in a memoir is critical to making a story something a reader can't put down. Taking the time and thought to establish the plot and join the stories to it is an essential part of building a worthy memoir.

The writer must make decisions as to what is relevant to the story, and what events happened around the same time as the narrative, but are unrelated to the story the writer wants to tell.

For example, if a person wants to write a memoir about going on a quest to see the Dali Lama, the writer's cat at home getting a new collar is not necessarily relevant to the story of seeing the Dali Lama.

As the story is written, it will become more clear as to which events and experiences are relevant to the story being told, and which are not.

However, don't throw away the cut, unused pieces of text or stories. Some episodes that may not be major can sometimes be used later on as creative devices to reflect on the major events that have occurred or are occurring within the context of the story. You would be wise to paste those cut pieces into another file in your folder, perhaps simply labeled, "cut pieces."

You never know when one of them might fit in a spot in this work or a new one and be exactly what you needed.

College writing taught me there is no such thing as completely bad writing. If it doesn't work in one document, it might work in another with a few tweaks and adaptations. I never throw away a story.

On the other hand, if you've worked and reworked a paragraph or small story in your memoir, but it doesn't seem to move the plot along, or fit where you're determined to put it, cut it out. This is a serious clue that perhaps it doesn't belong there. Put it in your "cut pieces" file if you like, and maybe it will work somewhere else. But for this story, cut it out.

Give yourself a limited time to stress over something that isn't working.

A time to reflect

Jot down some notes, doodle, reflect...

Memories

Chapter 8

Editing

Not everything you write will be gold. Some writers call a first draft "puking on paper." This means you just write and write and write, hardly paying attention to how you're saying it, just say it. Tell it all.

When the first writing is finished, and after you've pulled things together enough to have a good first draft of your story, start back at the beginning, scrutinizing and analyzing. Weed out what's unnecessary and repetitive. Take out pieces which don't seem to fit. Be sure to put them in your "cut pieces" file because you never know when you might need a filler.

Then do it again.

Not every instance of your existence is worth noting. If an event isn't part of a flowing transition into another, it doesn't have to make it to the page. Include only what gets you to your end point without meandering from your path.

Every good author knows or needs to know he or she cannot sufficiently do a final edit of their own work. If this will be a published book, particularly, you *must* find an editor who will honestly critique your book. You can use friends, but remember they may not be comfortable in critiquing it effectively and honestly in order to be "helpful" to improve or enhance the value of the content.

When you give your work to someone to edit, ask that person specific questions, such as looking at your focus, cohesiveness, structure, and format. Responses from them about the content of the document will be more helpful than comments about your writing. Tell your editor who your target market is, and ask this person if they honestly think your work will appeal to that market.

Proofreading is not the same as editing, and must be done by a different professional:

- Editing is looking at all aspects of the content of the writing, including grammar, punctuation, and word use, as well as how it flows and properly tells the story.
- Proofreading is finding misused and misspelled words (and pulling out excess words like *that* and *very*, and other overused words or terms. This second pair of eyes can find things the editor missed—and point them out.

Proofreading is best done when the story or book is in the final draft stage, including formatting, in order to watch for typesetting/flow issues.

A time to reflect

Jot down some notes, doodle, reflect...

Memories

Chapter 9

Naming Your Story

Don't worry about naming the story early on. When you get into it, the name may become obvious. If not, think more about the plot or why you're writing the story.

My own memoir's name came after quite a bit of thought. I was calling it *A Lifetime of Eating*. Boring, yes. I thought some more and came up with *Musing and Munching* which seemed to nail it.

Here are a few examples of cleverly named memoirs:

- *Hotel on the Corner of Bitter and Sweet*; Jamie Ford about life in the mid-1940s when America's Japanese on the West Coast were put in camps.
- Frank McCourt wrote *Angela's Ashes*, about his poverty-stricken life in Ireland, and *Teacher Man*, about teaching school in New York.

- *Valleys of Death, A Memoir of the Korean War*, by Bill Richardson and Kevin Mauer.
- *Cartwheels in a Sari; A Memoir of Growing up Cult*, Jayanti Tamm.
- *Half-Broke Horses*, and *The Glass Castle* by Jeanette Walls.
- *I Know Why the Caged Bird Sings*, Maya Angelou, about her life of poverty, bigotry, and pain.

Cover and Design

How the book will be published or printed determines the cover and design. You can work with a designer or your printer or publisher to see what works for your type of story. Be aware that cover art can be expensive and photography must be credited to the owner.

Pictures are great in a life story, and can be inserted within the text as appropriate. There is a major cost difference between black and white and color, and collaboration with your printer or publisher is necessary. Also, if pictures are taken by someone other than yourself, they must be credited to the photographer, and you must get written permission to use them.

A time to reflect

Jot down some notes, doodle, reflect...

Memories

Chapter 10

Build Your Writing Muscle

A writer needs to develop his or her writing muscle, and that muscle needs exercise to perform well. Just like doing yoga or physically working out in another way, the writing muscle needs to be developed and strengthened.

Set a daily goal (maybe three or four days a week) of writing 200, 500, or even 1,000 words. Set aside a regular time, like early morning, or late night, or whatever time works best in your life. Remember the flinch-worthy statement, "puking on paper," and just write, without concern for proper spelling or grammar or format. Just write.

The key is to be disciplined. Don't worry about making what you write perfect. Focus on getting the story out, and you can do the polishing later. Above all, relax. Memoir is the easiest type of writing to do well. You've already done the research. You've lived your life, and you are intimately familiar with every character. You know what happened and it's buried in your memory. Now you must dig it out and tell your story.

As Jeanette Walls says about writing a memoir,

> *"It's honestly sharing what you think, feel, and have gone through. If you can do that effectively, then somebody gets the wisdom and benefit of your experience without having to live it."*

A time to reflect

Jot down some notes, doodle, reflect...

Memories

Chapter 11

How to Publish/print Your Story

When you reach the end of the road in writing- and rewriting-your story, and you feel it's ready for publication, many options are available for publishing or printing it.

To begin the decision, go back to my first questions: Who is the story for, and why are you writing it? As mentioned before, the answers can change throughout the writing process. Maybe your first view of your story is of a beautifully bound hard-cover book with an eye-catching cover, that screams, "Buy Me!" to strolling readers in bookstores. Your second view could be more modest...and realistic.

Publishing and printing depend on the number of copies you want to give away or sell. Will you hand your story only to members of your family? Do you expect it to be available in book stores?

Also, do you want your story available in only hard copy or an e-book readable on iPad or Kindle?

Here are a few options for your story:

- You can print your story with your own computer and make copies at printing places like Kinkos.
- You can start sending it to agents and publishers and begin gathering rejection slips. Years ago, two newspaper book reviewers, and others, advised me that self-publishing is the way to go for new writers. In today's world, only the biggest names get published by the big publishing houses.
- You can contact a printer and work with them to print your story. Many, like FuzionPrint of Burnsville, Minnesota, will work with you on available options. (Ann Aubitz, of FuzionPrint has written a booklet called *Publishing: Frequently Asked Questions*, which describes publishing options and requirements in detail. Contact her at Ann@FuzionPrint.com)
- You can buy self-publishing packages from a variety of publish-on-demand publishers. This is how I published my first book when I knew absolutely nothing about writing or publishing. I started asking other writers how to do it, including some quite successful people, and I was advised to self-publish. I found Xlibris on the Internet for my first book and by pure luck got a good package, for about $1,500 in 2009. My third book, about WWII, was published by

Archway, the self-publishing arm of Simon and Schuster. The cost was comparable to my first book. I chose them because they have a large worldwide presence, and my book would appeal to buyers in other countries.
- Most print-on-demand printers/publishers will make your book available on Amazon and Barnes and Noble online, and book stores and individuals can order it there. You must purchase copies from the publisher to sell on your own.

An example of true self-publishing success is Lisa Genova, who wrote *Still Alice*, a novel about Alzheimer's disease. She couldn't get a publisher to buy her book, so she self-published. Her book became so successful, it was eventually bought up by Simon and Schuster and became a *New York Times* best seller, and then was made into a major motion picture. Success is truly a possibility if one is patient and willing to work for it.

You can find many inexpensive self-publishing options on the Internet, like Create Space, which is owned by Amazon. Do your research, ask others who have published, and compare answers, to find what works best for you.

A time to reflect

Jot down some notes, doodle, reflect...

Memories

Chapter 12

Good Luck and Keep Writing

This is a brief overview of memoir or life story writing, and my fervent hope is to inspire you to start capturing your own memories for your loved ones.

The tears on the faces of families of hospice patients when they receive their loved ones' finished stories that I've written, are burned into my own memory. Without exception, the families have never heard some of the stories, and they are touched and grateful.

One example is a man whose adult children are all professionals with advanced degrees. They thought it was foolish to have me capture this executive's story because they thought there wasn't anything new to learn about his life. They believed it had all been captured already. At the man's funeral, a daughter came to me, saying, "Thank you so much for writing our dad's story. On the very first page, I learned five things about his life that I didn't know."

A woman who started writing her own story after attending one of my classes on how to do it, showed the story to her son and daughter. There were exclamations and tears, and sincere gratitude for capturing memories which the family would never have known without the story. It became a priceless family legacy to be handed down through generations to come.

If you need more information, full college classes are available, or look for other books on the subject: one is by Mary Karr who wrote *The Art of Memoir*. Another is Tristine Rainer, author of *Your Life as Story*. William Zinsser's book is called: *Writing About Your Life*.

The more you know, the easier the process becomes and the more likely you are to do it.

My web site is gloriavan.com, and I love to hear from readers through the Contact page on the site. It goes directly to my email and we can chat.

Most of all, I hope you start writing.